A Note of Love to My Son

_____

_____

_____

D1451140

For the son I love with all my hearts, Michael.
– Sally Huss

Published in Nashville, Tennessee, by Tommy Nelson™, a division of Thomas Nelson, Inc. Managing Editor: Laura Minchew; Editor: Tama Fortner; Art Director: Karen Phillips

Scripture quotations are from the *International Children's Bible, New Century Version*, copyright © 1986, 1988 by Word Publishing. Used by permission.

Library of Congress Cataloging-in-Publication Data

Huss, Sally.
    I love you with all my hearts : the many ways a mother loves her son / written and illustrated by Sally Huss.
        p.   cm.
    Summary: A mother describes all the different ways she loves her son.
    ISBN 0-8499-5886-5
    [1. Mothers and sons—Fiction. 2. Love—Fiction. 3. Stories in rhyme.] I. Title.
    PZ8.3.H955Il   1998
    [E]—dc 21   98-36931
                                                                                  CIP
                                                                                  AC

Printed in the United States of America
98 99 00 01 02 03 QBH 9 8 7 6 5 4 3 2 1

I Love You with all My Hearts

Written and Illustrated by

Sally Huss

The many ways a mother loves her son

Tommy
NELSON

Thomas Nelson, Inc.
Nashville

There are many ways to love,
and many ways of love
That you may not have thought of.

Within each person,
   there is a heart for every job or task
      For which a heart
         could possibly be asked.

Here are some of the
   ways I have loved you . . .
And the ways I still do.

When you were a baby,
I gave you baths and kept you dry.
I fed you when you
were hungry
and soothed you
when you'd cry.

I made you wear jackets
and hats on cold days,
And fixed you chicken soup
on days when a
cold stays.

There was always a bandage
for a scratch or bump,
And a hug from your mother
when your throat got a lump.

I made sure you had plenty of sleep
and lots of fresh air.
These were the ways I loved you.
These were my hearts of . . . Care.

Then there were times of joy.
You were so full of fun
for such a little boy.

You liked to be tickled
from your head to your toes.

And you liked to dress up
in your cowboy clothes.

You dared the ocean to catch you
    when we were at the beach.
And when it did,
    you would let out the loudest screech.

A trip on Boulder Mountain
brought screams and squeals
and giggles long after.

These were the ways I loved you.
These were my hearts of . . . Laughter.

Now and then there were hard times,
  which brought tears sometimes.
When we had to move,
  and you and your best friend
  said goodbye,

As you hugged each other,
  I thought I'd cry.

And as we left our old home
with all of its memories, too,
I knew this was hard on you.

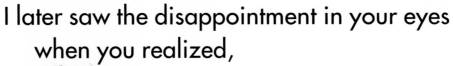

I later saw the disappointment in your eyes
when you realized,

That we did not have the money
    to buy a bike –
    we found one to borrow.

These were the ways I loved you.
These were my hearts of . . . Sorrow.

Through weekends and school days, you have grown in so many wonderful ways.

Being a leader by nature,
you have been a help
to your teacher,

Making sure the work got done
while your group was having fun.

And happily you have learned
     to share your games and toys
With the neighborhood
     girls and boys.

And when your grandfather came to stay,
You even figured out a game
for him to play.

Then you surprised us all at Christmastime
as you stood upon the stage,
Playing Tiny Tim's father
and acting well beyond your age.

Your grandmother and I
    were so touched, we cried.
These were the ways I loved you.
These were my hearts of . . . Pride.

Times of peacefulness
   found their way into our lives,
Often, when you
   were about to close your eyes.

At night we spoke of true things,
  of important things,
Of God's love,
  and blessings from above.

There were quiet picnics under trees,
When we watched the ants
and studied leaves.

And after lunch,
    when all the work was done,
I looked down on you,
    my sleeping son,
      an arm around your lamb of fleece.
These were the ways I loved you.
These were my hearts of . . . Peace.

For these reasons and more –
including all life's other parts –
I want you to know
that now and forever,

I love you with all my hearts!

My Hearts of Care

Love is patient and kind. – *1 Corinthians 13:4*

We love because God first loved us. – *1 John 4:19*

My children, our love should not be only words and talk. Our love must be true love. And we should show that love by what we do. – *1 John 3:18*

My Hearts of Laughter

I have told you these things so that you can have the same joy I have. I want your joy to be the fullest joy. – *John 15:11*

There is a right time for everything. . . . There is a time to cry and a time to laugh. – *Ecclesiastes 3:1, 4*

Your words came to me, and I listened carefully to them. Your words made me very happy. I was happy because I am called by your name.
– *Jeremiah 15:16*

My Hearts of Sorrow

Those who are sad now are happy. God will comfort them.
– *Matthew 5:4*

In this world you will have trouble. But be brave! I have defeated the world!
– *John 16:33*

And we also have joy with our troubles because we know that these troubles produce patience. And patience produces character, and character produces hope. – *Romans 5:3–4*